I0473130

The Best Darn Invention Marketing Book!

Vital Information for the Aspiring Inventor

By: James M. Lowrance © 2010

TABLE OF CONTENTS:

CHAPTER ONE

Researching the Market Value of Inventions

Determining the Worth of a New Product Idea

When an invention is believed to have potential for being successfully developed into a marketable product, there are questions that help to determine that evaluation.

While an invention can appear to have potential when considered on face-value, it is in an inventor's best interest to research the market potential of a new product idea, the best possible, before investing further time and expense into its development. There are several basic areas that should be considered in this process of evaluating an invention, as addressed in the subheadings that follow.

Does the Invention Solve a Problem?

This is always a major question when evaluating an invention because solving a problem is the basic purpose behind all inventions.

4

It needs to eliminate a step that adds difficulty in accomplishing something or in making that step easier for those using the invention.
Some of the ways a product-invention helps to solve a problem include the following.

• makes a common task easier
• eliminates a step in accomplishing a task
• adds enjoyment to a task
• provides a convenience when performing a task

If for example an invention is in the area of household cleaning products the invention should solve a problem or add a convenience in that area. A product that makes it easier to empty a full vacuum cleaner bag, a dishwasher additive that improves the cleaning action on dishes and an attachment for a bathtub-shower cleaning brush that allows reaching better from a standing position, would all be examples of household cleaning products that solve a problem for consumers.

If the invention only solves a minor problem that most people are not concerned about, an inventor may feel it is not worth pursuing further.

5

If it solves a problem that is concerning to consumers who are obviously looking for a solution, this may indicate that is has real market value. This is the basic appeal that would create sales and by determining how important it is in solving a problem or adding a convenience, this can also help to determine its potential market value.

Does the Invention have a Wide Appeal?

Even when a product has a definite problem solving ability, this does not necessarily determine how well it will sell on the market. If for example, an invention is a chew-toy for dogs with sensitive teeth that would be very desirable for owners of dogs suffering with this problem.

It does however need to be determined if there are only a small number of dogs who have this problem or if there are potentially large numbers of them.

A company, who already manufactures dog chew-toys, could add this type product to their line and it would possibly be worthwhile for them to do so.

An inventor however would likely only benefit to a small degree should he license the invention (to receive royalty-percentage payments) to a dog chew-toy company due to limited sales compared to products that would benefit all dogs in general. In these cases an inventor needs to determine the cost to develop an invention into a presentable product for pet toy companies, versus the amount that might be paid in royalties under a License Agreement or for an outright sale of the invention. If the cost to develop it is not higher than the expected profit that would be made, the invention might be worth pursuing further.

Can the Invention be Manufactured at a Reasonable Cost?

Determining the cost to manufacture an invention consists of materials needed to make a finished product and in the manufacturing process. Some inventions have parts that are already available through other manufacturers and can be incorporated into the finished product, to reduce some of the cost. If there are however, parts that require special tooling or molds, this must be factored into the manufacturing cost.

If an inventor plans to license his invention and not self-manufacture it, the "Licensee" (company that will manufacture it) can conduct research for using the most affordable materials needed that still retain quality for the finished product. If an inventor plans to self-market the product-invention, he would still need to have manufacturers helping him, to conduct studies on costs to afford-ably but effectively manufacture a finished product on a timely basis.

Can the Invention be Packaged Afford-ably?

Packaging is a major factor in both protecting a product from damage and in attracting consumers with sales appeal. Most product-inventions can be packaged for sale feasibly, so that the cost of the packaging doesn't raise the final retail price too high for consumers to afford it. There are however cases in which a product has multiple parts that must be wrapped in protective materials inside of its main container.

Products can also be heavier than average and require stronger, more expensive materials to protect and package them.

8

An inventor needs to determine if he or a manufacturer he may license or sell his invention to, can package his product-invention efficiently and afford-ably, so that it can still be offered at a desirable retail price. This may require researching the cost of packaging materials and the cost to a manufacturer to complete this packaging, using similar products they already package as a guideline.

Once the cost of packaging is reasonably determined, an inventor must then combine this cost with that required for manufacturing the invention itself, to determine if an appealing final retail for consumers can still be achieved. If one type of packaging cannot achieve this, an inventor may need to look into alternative ways to package his invention.

These questions and considerations are useful in evaluating the worth in pursuing marketing of a product-invention. It is, however, also important to protect the invention as the inventor goes through this evaluation process by making sure they do not disclose details of it to anyone before they have obtained proper patent protection.

The Best Darn Invention Marketing Book!

CHAPTER TWO

Preparing for Invention Submission

Patent Pending and Production Costs

When an inventor is planning to submit an invention to industry for outright sale or for licensing or to market it himself, there is vital information needed to proceed. Being fully prepared for submitting an invention to companies with potential interest for marketing it or to directly launch a marketing campaign for an invention is very important. The two main areas of importance are protecting an invention and thoroughly researching costs involved in developing an invention for retail sale readiness. These are essential factors needed for new product marketing.

Patent Protection

The U.S. Patent & Trademark Office (USPTO) warns that not obtaining a patent pending status for an invention within one year of public disclosure can result in denial of a patent application.

The Best Darn Invention Marketing Book!

It is highly recommended that an invention not be disclosed publicly by an inventor before patent protection is in place. While some inventors desire to first see if there is public interest for their product-invention before going the expense of a patent pending, it is very risky business to test-market without one.

Provisional Patent Program

One cost-effective route for protecting an invention that has been made available by the USPTO is the "Provisional Patent Program" (also covered in SECTION ONE). Once an inventor has conducted a thorough patent search on their own or through a patenting agent or attorney, it can then be submitted for a 1-year provisional patent. The cost for small entities (individuals and companies with 500 employees or less) is only $110.00, as of the year 2009. The patent can be allowed to lapse after the initial term with no further obligation or an inventor can resubmit the invention for a full-term patent of 14 years. This gives an inventor time to develop and test market his product-invention before he invests in further patent expenses.

Manufacturing Costs

Having a new product idea can be exciting, especially if the product-invention is unique and will genuinely solve a problem or offer a needed-convenience to consumers who will purchase it. Even if an inventor does not directly sell an invention, having accurate costs figured to manufacture a shelf-ready product with the best possible accuracy is essential.

This is so all levels of markup at the following levels can be calculated as accurately as possible:

• Distributor price
• Wholesale price
• Sales rep commissions
• Final retail

(Note: Some manufacturers choose not to sell to distributors or pay sales rep commissions but strictly sell at a single wholesale price to retailers.)

This will let the inventor know how competitive a finished, packaged product will be on the market.

It is information potential licensees also require (whether researched by them or the inventor) in order to seriously consider marketing an invention under a royalty agreement with a licensor (one offering rights to an invention).

Competitive Final Retail

If the final retail of a new product is undesirable to the consumer, this can override their recognition of how useful the product would be to them because of non-affordability or lack of cost-effectiveness.
Costs may need to be cut back in the following areas to keep the final retail competitive:

• Manufacturing process
• Materials
• Packaging

(Inventors who market their own inventions must also consider promotional and advertising costs.) This may require research to find the most cost effective sources and resources to obtain best possible prices while retaining a necessary quality and attractiveness for a product-invention.

13

Having these costs in place can help an inventor go much further when submitting an invention to potential licensees, potential investors and even potential retail store outlets and chains.

CHAPTER THREE

Conducting a Preliminary Patent Search

Searching Online before Securing Professional Assistance

A patent search can confirm the originality of a new invention or reveal that a similar invention has already been protected under an existing patent or patent-pending.

While an inventor can conduct a patent search on his own, there are also patent agents and attorneys who can assist in this for a fee. Searching online can help inventors locate patent search assistance so that it is conducted professionally. This will offer assurance that it has been done thoroughly and completely.

Some inventors may wish to conduct their own preliminary patent search first, before paying for professional assistance. The subheadings that follow can help inventors know how to conduct a preliminary patent search.

Search the Shelves and Catalogs of Retail Outlets

While this step isn't technically part of a patent search, it can help confirm the value in conducting one. It might also reveal to an inventor that no further search is needed if the invention already exists on the market. A more thorough preliminary patent search would not be necessary; if an inventor discovers that his invention or one that is very similar is already being marketed by someone else. As a first step in establishing the originality of a product invention and in determining if more thorough search is merited, it's a good idea to make sure a product-idea is not already widely available in major chain stores or in major catalog outlets.

Conduct a Search on Major Search Engines

This is a another preparatory step in getting ready for conducting an actual patent search through the United States Patent & Trademark Office (USPTO). There are websites that are not actually connected to the USPTO, yet still index patented inventions.

Some of them also include listings of non-patented inventions on the search engines, as part of their services to inventors. By conducting an online search on Google, an inventor can better-establish the need to do a more detailed and thorough search on the USPTO website. Google in-fact now has a search engine called "Google patents beta".

Other major search engines in addition to Google include the following:

• Yahoo.com
• Ask.com
• MSN.com
• AolSearch.com
• HotBot.com
• AltaVista.com
• Gigablast.com

If, for example, an inventor believes he has a new, unique type of windshield wiper for automobiles, he can use several variations of search terms that describe the product-invention. It might also yield more results to include the word "patent" in the search.

This step not only helps to locate any pages of patented inventions that might be similar to a new invention, but also displays results on any non-patented products in general that might already be on the market.

A widely marketed product of similar purpose or design might pose too much competition for a new invention and might be a deciding factor against a further search using the USPTO website.

Searching Patents on the USPTO Website

The value in a more thoroughly conducted patent search is in working toward getting patent protection for an original invention by following up with a patent application. But it also helps prevent an inventor from infringing upon another patent which could make them legally liable for damages if it results in loss of sales or threatens the originality of an existing patented invention.

Inventors or their agents/attorneys can go online and visit the "USPTO's Index to the United States Patent Classification System".

This online source of granted patents and patent-pending inventions lists inventions of every kind that have been submitted through applications, in alphabetical categories.

Conducting a thorough patent search, following a preliminary one or even as a first-step toward gaining protection for inventions, takes time but can be well worth the effort to establish the originality and patentability of them.

CHAPTER FOUR

The Valuable USPTO Provisional Patent Program

Full Invention Protection for One Year

The U.S. Patent & Trademark Office's - Provisional Patent Program offers patent protection for one year while inventors develop their inventions. This program allows time for establishing the value of inventions, before investing in more permanent type patents. This is an important way to help new inventors reserve more of their funds for invention development, rather than needing more up-front money to invest in patents and before having the opportunity to fully test-market their inventions.

One Year Length Provisional Patents

The Provisional Patent Program (PPP) which was established by the USPTO in the year 1995 has in one sense replaced a former program discontinued by the USPTO that was called the "Disclosure Document Program" (DDP).

The DDP was a method offered to establish an invention's "date of conception" but offered no real protection and was discontinued in the year 2007.

A provisional patent offers an established date of conception for inventions and much more. This includes a trial period for test marketing and selling an invention for one year, before an inventor follows through with one of three more permanent types of patents. Continuing with longer-term patents is optional under the PPP and an inventor may instead allow it to lapse if he feels his invention does not merit further patenting.

The three longer term patents which are 14 years in duration include the following:

• design patents (design for an article of manufacture)
• industrial patents (a new and useful process of manufacture or composition of matter)
• plant patent (new asexually produced variety of plant).

Securing a "Patent Pending" Status

Formerly, when inventors sent their invention-descriptions in to the USPTO under the Disclosure Document Program, they would do so to establish a "date of conception," meaning proof of the date in which they established having invented it. This program, however, was not a protection for the invention as a provisional patent is and also did not allow for the inventor placing the "patent pending" notation on their invention; it's packaging and promotional materials. This is the advantage that the still affordable provisional patent has over the former, lower cost DDP.

A Cost of $105.00 for Small Entities

The USPTO offers provisional patents to small entities, meaning individuals or companies that have less than 500 employees, for a nominal fee of only $105.00 (please check the USPTO website for price updates). This is a very cost-effective price because an inventor is allowed to test market his invention for one year after notification that they have received and accepted a PPP application.

The Best Darn Invention Marketing Book!

If during the one year, an inventor discovers that the invention does not merit following through with a more permanent patent, at additional costs, he can allow the term to expire and forfeit the option to continue the patenting processes. If an inventor decides his invention is not worth the obtaining of a longer term patent (14 years), he can simply allow the provisional patent to lapse and he will have no further patenting costs or obligations with the USPTO. If, however, the value of the invention is proven during the one year grace period, the inventor may choose to invest further, to obtain a longer-term patent.

Opportunity for License Agreements

A major value of the one-year grace period provided by the PPP is that the worth/value of the invention can be established, with a much-lower risk of theft of the inventor's product-invention. It is also valuable in that an inventor may pursue a licensing (royalty agreement) during the one year grace period.

If any further patenting is done, it would be the responsibility of the "licensee" (if specified contractually).

This means the party paying royalties on sales for marketing an invention under a License Agreement, would be responsible for patent updates, should an inventor ("licensor") secure a licensing for his invention before the one year period has expired.

See the link in the "Sources" section below, that goes to the USPTO webpage, which gives detailed information about the PPP. The page also gives instructions on how to apply for a provisional patent and the address for sending applications and payment, to secure a provisional patent status for an invention.

CHAPTER FIVE

Test Marketing Inventions Effectively

Determining the Potential of New Products

When an inventor has a new invention that he wants to be certain will sell well on the market, he can take steps that help determine the marketability of the invention.

Test marketing a new product-invention not only gives potential buyers the opportunity to see how much demand there is for a product, but also gives the inventor the opportunity to determine how much further time and investment an invention merits.

It is important before using any of the methods listed in the subheadings below, that an inventor first secure proper patent protection for an invention that will be test-marketed as discussed in the previous chapters.

The Value in Test Marketing New Product-Inventions

The benefits that are accomplished through test marketing product-inventions include the following.

• to get an idea of how well a new product will be received by the public
• to see if there is a demand for it in the marketplace
• to determine if there will be repeat customers for a new product
• to gain the interest of buyers at retail chain stores and outlets

Display an Invention at Trade Shows

There are many trade shows that offer booth space for displaying and selling new products. If for example, an invention is in the hardware category, he can look for scheduling of trade shows for hardware products in his area or in areas he is willing to travel to. A great way to find information on trade shows is to go online and use search terms such as "upcoming hardware trade shows".

To find ones being held in a particular state or city, one can simply add the name of the city and/or state in the search term.

By attending trade shows and displaying a product-invention, one can get an idea of how well it will be received by the public, by observing how many people attending them stop by a display booth to look at a new product. This also gives the opportunity to ask attendees what they think about a product, if they would use it and if they see any features of the product they would prefer to see modified. After attendance at a number of these type shows, one would then be able to compare notes on them and have a better idea of how the product will be received by the general public, once it becomes available on the market.

Offer a Product-Invention through Telemarketing Sales

There are local cable advertising programs available in most cities that allow one to advertise in a limited area for a lower cost than regional or national advertising will cost.

Most of them also offer production services and can produce a semi-professional telemarketing spot for a product-invention.

An inventor would also need to obtain a toll-free ordering phone line, for taking orders, which are now available at a low cost or on a charge-per-call basis. Some major phone companies that provide basic phone service will also add a toll free phone line to existing basic service at no additional charge.

Some T.V. shows have unsold advertising spots that they might be willing to offer in exchange for a percentage of sales a product generates from an ad.

This is called a "P.I." arrangement meaning one agrees to pay the show running the ad a percentage of each sell or "per inquiry" that it generates. By offering a product-invention for sale in a T.V. ad, one is often able to see if there is a demand for it in the marketplace.

Conduct Surveys of Consumers Regarding a Product-Invention

To survey potential buying-consumers, one needs to compose a survey form, with lines for them to sign. The document would simply need to inquire as to whether a consumer would like to see a new product available at their local store. These surveys, once completed, can also be presented to potential buyers of the product whose interest in carrying it in their stores is often heightened by any public interest that is shown.

If one is trying to get the interest of a particular store-chain or outlet, wording the survey so that public interest is shown in seeing a new product specifically available in that store can add to its effectiveness. These type surveys can be conducted at trade shows or booth shows of any kind but can also be conducted at stores where one wants to generate interest. This would of course require that there is permission granted to conduct the survey on the store premises. A large list of consumers signing this type of survey can generate more interest with buyers who see the respondents as potential repeat customers for a new product.

Ask Permission to Test a Product-Invention in Stores

If one is trying to gain the interest of a chain-store for example, an appointment can be made with the corporate buyer and request the opportunity to test a new product in one or up to a few of their stores. If permission to test market a new product in a limited number of stores is granted, it gives an opportunity to monitor the sales, to see if the product can be expanded in the chain.

This of course would be dependent upon how well the test period goes with a product. It might also be a good idea to advertise the new product in the cities it is available in for the test, by placing ads in local newspapers. To gain the interest of a buyer for test marketing a product, one could also offer the new product at a discounted price and let the buyer know that advertising will be obtained for the authorized store(s) during the test.

The preceding subheadings offer general guidelines for several methods that can help determine the market value of a new product-invention.

The Best Darn Invention Marketing Book!

An inventor would however want to proceed with any test marketing, with caution, making sure that public exposure of an invention is done at the best possible timing. It is also important while attempting to determine the sales potential of a new product, that any contracts or agreements involved in the process are carefully considered and researched, which may require the assistance of legal counsel in some cases.

CHAPTER SIX

The Invention License Agreement Option

Receiving Royalty Payments from a Manufacturer

An inventor has two options to choose from to proceed with getting an invention marketed, self-marketing or a License Agreement.

These two options should be investigated and researched if both are being considered. The advantage of self-marketing is in the fact that an inventor has potential to a make a higher profit margin through direct sales of an invention. The advantage in licensing an invention is in the fact that despite a lower profit being made, the expense and labor in the marketing effort is that of the manufacturer obtaining the rights.

Self-Marketing an Invention

With the self-marketing option, an inventor will be responsible for every aspect of the marketing process, from top to bottom.

This would include getting the following items completed.

• obtaining a patent pending and/or trademark registration
• getting packaging designed and printed for merchandising through retail outlets
• setting up a manufacturing facility or obtaining the services of a manufacturer
• securing product liability insurance required by retail outlets

In order to have a finished, packaged product ready to ship to merchandisers, retail outlets and distributors, these requirements must be met. There are many other responsibilities that must be completed as well, in order to have a product ready for launching on the market. These are the things to consider when looking into the self-marketing option.

The License Agreement Option

The other option would be for the inventor to offer the product-invention for licensing, to a manufacturer.

This would be a company who can take care of these issues and simply pay a "royalty" percentage from sales of the finished product. The name for a contract of this type that would be entered into is a "License Agreement."

The product owner/inventor would be the "licensor," simply meaning the party granting the rights and the manufacturer entering into the agreement, to market the product-invention, would be the "licensee," simply meaning the party who is being granted these rights.

The Advantages of Licensing

What are the other advantages in licensing a product-invention, when compared to self-marketing? One major advantage is that all of the previously mentioned items, needing completed in order to get the product ready for marketing, would be at the licensee's time and expense. This usually excludes the expense for the first stages of patenting, since most inventors choose to get at least a "patent pending" status (pending approval for a full-term patent) before public exposure of their invention.

There are some inventors who actually license their inventions with the condition included that the licensee/manufacturer pay for the securing of a patent pending. In cases like these however, it is important that an inventor proceed cautiously and with use of "Non-Disclosure - Non-Use Agreements," signed prior to allowing review of the invention. This type of agreement states that the reviewing party agrees not to use the invention, in any way or to disclose it, to third parties, without prior written consent of the inventor.

The problem with proceeding without a patent however is that manufacturers will have reason to question an invention's potential. They may feel that if the inventor is not willing to first apply for a patent pending, before offering it for licensing, that they may lack real confidence in the invention. If the inventor doesn't believe in it enough to apply for a patent, why should they?

The USPTO (U.S. Patent & Trademark Office) offers a 1-year patent pending under the "Provisional Patent Program" at a low cost of $110.00 for small entities (small companies and individuals).

With this and the effort of first conducting a patent search or having one completed, the expense of a patent pending can be held down to a minimum, prior to offering an invention for licensing.

The Licensee's Responsibilities

In addition to the advantage of expenses being the manufacturer's under a License Agreement, with the possible exception of a patent pending, another advantage is that all other responsibilities are also the licensee's. They are responsible for designing attractive packaging for the invention, getting product liability insurance secured for it and promoting the product-invention, through ongoing advertising.

The responsibilities in marketing a product are many but the advantage in licensing a product-invention, over self-marketing, is also in the fact that an existing manufacturer is already set up to accomplish these things. An inventor is simply granting the rights through a Licensing Agreement and is being paid a royalty percentage on any resulting sales.

Composing a License Agreement

It is important that proceeding with a prospective Licensing Agreement is done so with caution. An inventor must carefully consider every condition and term they wish to include in the agreement. Things to consider include the royalty percentage willing to be settled for and the initial term of agreement, meaning the length of time the initial term of the contract is to be for, in months or years.

An inventor will also want to include clauses/articles that protect them from law suits of any kind that might arise, as a result of the marketing practices of the manufacturing company.

The inventor would also need to be able to terminate the agreement in writing, in the event the manufacturer does not honor the agreement. Non-compliance can be due to non-payment of royalties or by not fulfilling a minimum sales requirement, in order for the agreement to remain in force, should this be included.

Terms would however need to be reasonable and workable and not so strict as to cause disinterest by potential manufacturers in entering into a contract to market an invention.

An inventor can study license agreements through search online and/or consult with an attorney who is experienced in composing and executing marketing contracts.

CHAPTER SEVEN

Pursuing License Agreements for Inventions

Successfully Securing Royalty Payments for New Products

A License Agreement is a contract that an inventor enters into with a marketing company that can manufacture and sell (market) his invention as mentioned previously. The information in the subheadings below can help an inventor know how to proceed with obtaining a License Agreement for his invention. It is important however that an inventor first take steps for protecting his invention under a patent pending before offering his invention for licensing. While this point has been repeated often, this is due to the great importance in not risking loss of rights to an original invention.

Making a Product-Invention Prototype

When manufacturing/marketing companies are approached with a new product idea by an inventor, they prefer to have a working model or sample design submitted to them.

This is called a "prototype" and an inventor can make the sample himself or if it is a somewhat complicated product, he can have a manufacturing firm or machine shop, sewing factory, etc. put one together for him.

It is better if an inventor is able to produce a prototype on his own if possible because this reduces the chances of early exposure of an invention and will save on the expense of having a prototype made by a manufacturer.

If an inventor has to use an outside source to get a sample (prototype) made, he should have them sign a "Non-Disclosure Non-Use Agreement," which is an agreement that simply states that upon disclosure of the invention to them, for the purpose of producing a prototype, they agree not to publicly disclose the invention to third parties or to make any further samples of the product for their own use.

The inventor has them sign such an agreement so that they do not expose an invention publicly sooner than it is ready to be launched onto the market.

Invention Submission Materials

It is important to look as professional in the efforts to secure a licensee/manufacturer as possible. An inventor needs to have a professional looking letter of request that is sent out to interest companies in seeing a presentation of a product/invention, with a letterhead at the top of it that includes contact information for interested parties.

It is important to put together the best submission materials possible. These type items can include the following:

• A brochure that describes and highlights an invention
• a demonstration video
• a chart that can be pointed to and referred to
• printed results from any positive test-marketing that has been done.

In other words, anything that presents an invention to a reviewing company in the best possible light is a good thing to have with when making a presentation for an invention.

License Agreement Proposal

Most manufacturers that express interest in an invention want the inventor to set their desired terms so that they can make a final consideration before entering into a License Agreement to market an invention. Manufacturers like to see inventors who know what they want out of their invention rather than having an inventor say to them, "Whatever you guys think." They prefer to have a more detailed proposal placed in front of them so that they can negotiate from that point.

An inventor can find a local attorney to help them compose a License Agreement proposal or they can find one on the internet using a search term such as "sample license agreements," etc. Once one has a general contract in hand, they can customize it to their liking.

The most likely term/condition that requires some time in negotiating with a licensee is the amount of royalty they will be required to pay on units sold for an invention under a licensing. Royalties paid on inventions can vary but according to some sources, a majority of inventions that are licensed receive a royalty between 2% and 10%.

The Best Darn Invention Marketing Book!

These suggestions can help an inventor to generally know how to pursue and prepare a License Agreement but one factor that is also of great importance is an inventor's ambition. A positive attitude and confidence in pursuing a License Agreement for an invention is a key factor. Inventors who remain confident, ambitious and who don't give up if they initially fail to interest the companies they first make presentations to, are the ones who succeed in eventually getting their inventions Licensed, to receive royalty payments from.

CHAPTER EIGHT

Methods for Licensing Inventions

Preparing New Product Submissions and
Presentations

The advantage for an inventor in licensing his
invention is that a manufacturer, marketing
company will agree to pay a small royalty
percentage on sales they achieve. Companies that
are potential licensees can be found by looking in
magazines or catalogs that feature products by
companies that are within an invention's field of
industry or one can go online and search using
terms on search engines that describe an invention
and find companies that way. It is important to
secure a patent pending before presenting an
invention to manufacturers for licensing
consideration.

Research Potential Licensee-Companies

The manufacturing/marketing company an
inventor licenses his invention to, is called the
"licensee" and the inventor or his agent is referred
to as the "licensor".

If an invention is in an industry such as pet supplies, fishing tackle, health & beauty aids, etc., then one simply gathers information on companies that are in the invention's field of industry, so that those who look reputable can be contacted about reviewing the new product-invention.

The advantages in securing a License Agreement for an invention include the following:

• Ongoing royalty payments
• marketing expenses are the licensee's
• an established company can gain wide exposure for inventions
• product liability and patent-related legal issues are the licensee's responsibility.

Following Up on Invention Submissions

When methods used for locating potential licensees yield lists of companies that look to be high quality and reputable in their industry, one can then contact them by written letter or by email to request an opportunity to submit an invention to their new product buyer.

One can then either follow-up on letters/emails with a phone call or it can be requested that contacted companies reply to the letter sent, to confirm receipt of it and/or interest in a more detailed submission. The advantage of mailed letters is that they can be sent return receipt, so that an inventor knows it was received, on a specific postmarked date.

It is usually more effective to state in a letter or email that it will be followed up with a phone call. When one receives responses from manufacturers interested in further reviewing an invention, one can either send a product sample/prototype and further written details about the invention or request an appointment to present the invention in person at their buying office.

Rehearsing and Timing Invention Presentations

A presentation should be practiced before making one in person. An inventor should be well prepared to make a presentation for their invention but should also insure that the presentation is timed, so that it does not exceed a reasonable time limit.

A presentation generally should not exceed 20 minutes in length because executive buyers with manufacturing companies are usually extremely busy and a shorter presentation can be effective and is usually the best approach.

A buyer can extend the length of a presentation if he chooses to, by asking questions after an inventor is done with the initial presenting.

Composing a License Agreement Proposal

An inventor should compose a sample license agreement that shows all of the terms and conditions that need to be included in the contract, leaving certain terms blank, such as the amount/percent of royalty that will be paid and the length/term of the contract in years that it is initially in force.

Having a proposal on-hand gives an inventor the readiness to negotiate terms, should a presentation meeting reach that stage of interest by a buyer.

License Agreement Terms and Conditions

An inventor may wish to set the term that a License Agreement is in force with a manufacturer (length of time) for only one or two years, with an option for renewal at the end of the term. This way, renewal depends upon the initial sales performance of the licensee. An inventor might also wish to include the condition of minimum sales that are accomplished per contract year by the manufacturer/licensee.

It might also be a good idea to include a clause in the contract that gives both inventor/licensor and the licensee the right to terminate the license agreement. This offers both parties a protective clause in the event for example that the licensee fails to pay royalties at the set contractual time periods or for other legitimate reasons.

A licensee might also respectfully terminate a License Agreement in the event they feel they would be unable to fulfill their obligations, so that the inventor/licensor can pursue better options.

Requiring Timely Royalty Payments

The royalty payment conditions can require royalties, to be calculated and paid, quarterly (4 times a year) or monthly, etc., and should the licensee become past-due in making royalty payments (by 10, 15 or 30 days, etc.); the licensor has the option to terminate the contract in writing – such as with a 15 or 30 day notice.

Inventors should take their time in pursuing License agreements carefully. Being in too much of a hurry to license an invention can result in bad decisions when entering into contracts that are binding and that must run their full terms unless terminated due to violations of terms. It is in an inventor's best interest to fully consider his options when entering into a License agreement and to do so with the help of an attorney if necessary.

CHAPTER NINE

My Invention Marketing Success Story Revisited

My Experience in Self-Marketing and Licensing Inventions

In the early 1980s, I co-invented a fishing tackle accessory, an attachment for fishing rod and reel combos with my brother-in-law we named "The Rod Floater". We saw the need for an invention that floats fishing rod and reel combos, after having near-drowning experiences with our own rod combos and after hearing the stories of other fishermen who had lost their own rod combos to watery graves, never to retrieve them. This inspired us to also add the catch phrase to the Rod Floater packaging; "A Life Vest For Your Fishing Rods!"

The Rod Floater is a very simple device, an 8-inch, cylinder-shaped piece of poly-foam material, similar to what you see water noodles and Nerf type toys made from.

It attaches to fishing rods, just above the rod handle, in the space above the fishing reel and just below the first rod eyelet.

We knew our invention had potential for the reasons I've stated plus the fact that children learning to fish and fishermen who are physically challenged are also at risk for dropping their rod combos overboard. To top it all off, my father-in-law had lost one of his own rod combos overboard, while trolling and having his fishing line snag on brush in the lake, which flipped his rod over the side, never to be retrieved in the deep water. With the Rod Floater, we knew that such mishaps would not end in tragedy because with our product invention, rods dropped overboard, would float on top of the water, allowing for easy retrieval of rod combos.

We eventually came out with Rod Floaters in bright yellow and orange, in addition to basic black so that fishermen are also able to spot rods dropped overboard, even at a significant distance. The bright colors are handy if a rod is dropped from a speeding boat and you have traveled a distance before being able to turn around and retrieve it.

If your rod is pulled overboard by a fish and he swims across the lake with it, it can be more easily located. Since marketing the Rod Floater starting in 1990, we have actually received letters from fishermen, including some from pro fishing guide services who were grateful to retrieve their rods after experiencing these very scenarios I have just described.

My Negative Invention Company Experience

My brother-in-law and I at the time were not familiar with the concept of invention companies but only had basic knowledge about them from seeing their ads in mechanics magazines. We decided we would contact one of them and request information. The one we contacted was one of the more publicized companies and upon receiving their information, we sent our invention concept to them in detail, on paper. They responded back to us promptly, assuring us that our invention had very broad potential. We decided to go with this invention company and paid for a "basic information package".

This consisted of them providing us a folder with market-potential estimates for our invention and professional line-art graphics, depicting our invention.

Upon receiving this basic information package, the invention company strongly suggested that we enter a contract with them, for a second step they would then undertake, to present our invention to industry for licensing it and if a licensing were successfully accomplished, we would receive royalty payments from sales of our product-invention. We did enter this second phase of their services, with a cost to us of several thousand dollars, the basic information package having already cost us several hundred dollars.

Beware of Invention Company Scams!

Let me say at the start of this paragraph in regard to invention companies, that not all of them practice bogus or false services, just to get fees from inventors but some invention companies are legitimate and sincere. In our case however, the invention company we entered into a contract with, was not completing the services they claimed to be providing.

We were able to determine this, by contacting many of the companies they claimed to be making submissions of our invention to and these companies made it very clear to us that they had never received the submissions.

At one point, the invention company also claimed they had found a corporation interested in marketing our invention and they eventually entered into a licensing agreement with them to market our invention. We were actually provided contracts to sign, in order for this corporation to manufacture and market our product-invention.

After more than a year following our signing of the licensing agreement, with no word from the invention company or the corporation/licensee, we inquired with the invention company as to the status of their marketing and were told that the corporation merged with another company and this newly-formed entity no longer wished to continue with the license agreement! We were devastated to say the least and at that point, asked for a release from the remaining time/term of our contract with the invention company and they granted us the release.

The lesson to learn from this example is to thoroughly investigate an invention company, their reputation, references and past history, before contracting with one to assist you with your invention!

A few months after the release from our contract with the invention company, I called the Chamber of Commerce in the city and state where this corporation who entered the license agreement with us was located. I was told that no such company ever existed and that if it had, regardless of their claimed merge with another company, they would have known about them. This confirmed my suspicions that began long before we asked for the release from our contract with the invention company, that they were indeed a bogus inventor's help-resource and not a legitimate invention company.

While I cannot give the company's name for obvious legal reasons, I will add that this experience having occurred over 20 years ago, could mean that the company has since reformed and may now be operating legitimately.

Then again, they may still be scamming sincere inventors out of their hard earned money to obtain illegitimate fees. If an inventor is determined to go the invention firm route, he should check for complaints against a company being considered, at the Better Business Bureau website.

There are also inventor information sources online, that actually list companies that are known to have committed scams. By conducting a search on Google or other search-engines using the term "Inventor Fraud", many pages of sources will appear that supply lists of companies to avoid. There is in fact one such resource called The National Inventor Fraud Center (NIFC) that directs inventors away from scam companies and toward any that are honest and reputable.

Despite our negative invention company experience, we eventually licensed the Rod Floater, in 1996 and have received monthly royalty checks from that time, to date. Some inventors prefer licensing to marketing on their own, which I have given detail-to, in the previous chapters.

Before getting the wonderful licensee we now have, we previously got the Rod Floater into Wal-Mart stores (regionally), Bass Pro Shops, Cabela's, Academy Stores, telemarketed on national T.V. shows and a national promotional premium deal with a major oil company, who promoted their outboard motor oil, using Rod Floaters as a giveaway in cases of the boat motor oil in the year 1992.

I invented and developed five other products in the outdoors sports industry and was able to get four more of these into Wal-Mart stores regionally as well before selling the products out-right to a company who still markets these as well.

It is my sincere wish that this eBook contributes to the success of many other inventors who help to give our world a brighter future through new and innovative inventions!

(END)